123 SESAME STREET

How Are You Feeling?

Naming Your Emotions with Sesame Street

Marie-Therese Miller

Lerner Publications ◆ Minneapolis

Everyone has big feelings! Learn how to name your emotions with your friends from *Sesame Street*. It's important for children to learn how to recognize and understand all their emotions so they can manage their feelings. They'll learn the importance of belly breaths, focusing, and so much more.

Sincerely,

The Editors at Sesame Workshop

TABLE OF CONTENTS

Everyone Has Big Feelings

We all have big feelings. These feelings have names.

I have big feelings too.

Let's learn how emotions look and how they feel.

Naming Your Emotions

People smile when they feel happy. They might even laugh.

Goodbyes can make you feel sad. Or you might be sad when a friend is unkind.

When I feel sad, the corners of my mouth turn down. Sometimes I also cry.

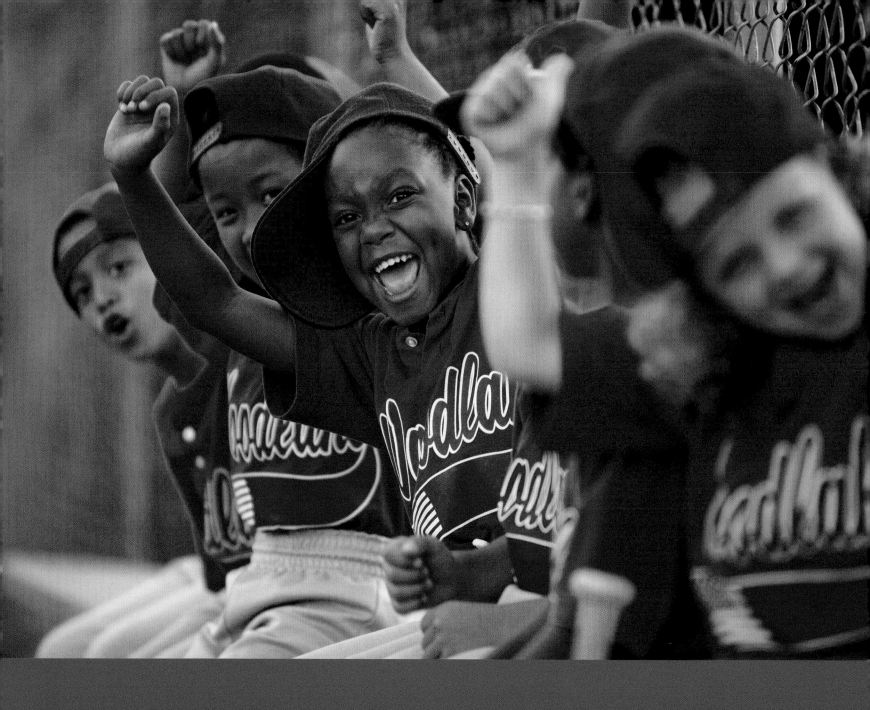

An excited person feels extra happy.
They might clap their hands or jump
up and down.

A disappointed person might frown. Their head might drop down, and their shoulders might droop.

Sometimes, you worry about what might happen. Maybe you worry about big things or small things.

When I feel worried, my muscles get tight and my tummy feels jumpy.

Something unexpected happens.

Your eyes and mouth open wide.

You feel surprised.

You argue with a friend. You are angry. Your cheeks feel hot and turn red. Your voice is loud.

Sometimes people feel scared. Maybe they are afraid of the dark.

When I'm scared, my heart beats fast and my muscles shake.

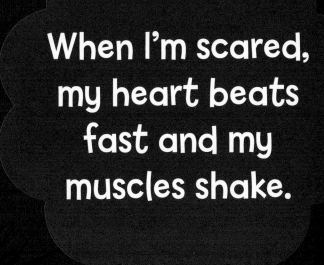

Maybe you feel jealous when someone else wins the race.

A person feels frustrated. They might not be able to do something yet, but they can keep trying.

When you feel proud, you stand up straight and hold your head up high.

Here are some ways to help you deal with your big feelings:

Take big belly breaths.

Count to ten.

Name everything around you that is green.

Walk away for a while.

Find somewhere quiet to sit.

Dance or bounce a ball.

Draw a picture or sing a song.

Talk to a friend.

Picture Glossary

cry: when tears fall from the eyes

frown: when the eyebrows are brought together and the corners of the mouth turn down

laugh: when a person makes sounds and smiles because something is funny

smile: when the mouth turns up at the corners to form a happy face

Learn More

Krekelberg, Alyssa. *Know Your Feelings: Recognizing Emotions*. Mankato, MN: Child's World, 2020.

Miller, Marie-Therese. *Caring with Bert and Ernie: A Book about Empathy*. Minneapolis: Lerner Publications, 2021.

Miller, Marie-Therese. *Feelings Like Mine*. Minneapolis: Lerner Publications, 2021.

Index

Photo Acknowledgments

Image credits: pixelheadphoto digitalskillet/Shutterstock, p. 1 (bottom); Monkey Business Images/Shutterstock, pp. 6, 30 (bottom left); Alinute Silzeviciute/Shutterstock, p. 8; Ariel Skelley/DigitalVision/Getty Images, p. 10; esthermm/Shutterstock, pp. 12, 30 (top right); SDI Productions/Getty Images, p. 14; Chaay_Tee/iStock/Getty Images, p. 16; Kris Ubach and Quim Roser/Getty Images, p. 18; Anatoliy Karlyuk/Shutterstock, p. 20; emholk/E+/Getty Images, p. 22; Juanmonino/Getty Images, p. 24; Klaus Vedfelt/DigitalVision/Getty Images, pp. 26, 30 (bottom right); Yuji Arikawa/Getty Images, p. 30 (top left).

Cover: Gelpi/Shutterstock; Roman Samborskyi/Shutterstock.

To John, Meghan, John Vincent, Erin, Elizabeth, Michelle, and Greyson, who give me all the big feelings

Lerner Publications Company
An imprint of Lerner Publishing Group, Inc.
241 First Avenue North
Minneapolis, MN 55401 USA

For reading levels and more information, look up this title at www.lernerbooks.com.

Main body text set in Tw Cen MT Std.
Typeface provided by Monotype Typography.

Editor: Amber Ross **Designer:** Emily Harris
Lerner team: Martha Kranes

Library of Congress Cataloging-in-Publication Data

Names: Miller, Marie-Therese, author.
Title: How are you feeling? : naming your emotions with Sesame Street / Marie-Therese Miller.
Description: Minneapolis : Lerner Publications, 2023. | Includes bibliographical references and index. | Audience: Ages 4–8 | Audience: Grades K–1
Identifiers: LCCN 2022011886 (print) | LCCN 2022011887 (ebook) | ISBN 9781728475752 (library binding) | ISBN 9781728486123 (paperback) | ISBN 9781728483986 (ebook)
Subjects: LCSH: Emotions—Juvenile literature. | Sesame Street (Television program)
Classification: LCC BF723.E6 M556 2023 (print) | LCC BF723.E6 (ebook) | DDC 152.4—dc23/eng/20220523

LC record available at https://lccn.loc.gov/2022011886
LC ebook record available at https://lccn.loc.gov/2022011887

Manufactured in the United States of America
1-52142-50605-7/20/2022